WHEN I WAS YOUR AGE

About the book:

Recent research has found that parents, not peers, are the primary value influence on youth during adolescence. This book explores family communication and its stumbling blocks, and how some of these stumbling blocks can become doors to better understanding.

About the author:

Joan Malerba-Foran is a youth outreach counselor in Connecticut. She has spoken to many youth groups over the past few years on peer/parent pressure, alcohol and other drugs, and other topics relevant to adolescents. This is her first publication.

WHEN I WAS YOUR AGE

Joan Malerba-Foran

Hazelden
Always, the pioneer

First published July, 1984

ISBN:0-89486-231-6

Printed in the United States of America.

Contents

Introduction

All adults were once children. All children will become adults. One has information the other needs. This would seem a perfect formula for family harmony.

Most often, an adolescent's need for information collides with the parents' desire to give it. The exchange is never as smooth as we would like. It's a tangled web of miscommunication and hurt feelings. Voices rise, tempers fly, threats are made, and each side retreats in frustration. But no matter how frustrated and angry everyone gets, we always come back for more. The deep need for love and understanding makes us try one more time to get the point across.

This book looks at some causes for this frustration. It breaks down key phrases we all say and hear so often and looks at the meaning hidden within. A lot more is happening than meets the ear. The surface of an argument is just a simple, and often misleading, version of what's going on underneath.

*　　*　　*

When a child reaches adolescence, there is usually a lot going on underneath. Adolescents want to forget they are children, and their parents often want to ignore the fact that their children are growing up.

Usually, the first response parents make to

a troubled son or daughter is an emotional one. Without meaning to, they turn their kids off with a lecture. An adolescent's response to a questioning parent is usually defensive. Children often expect an argument rather than a discussion.

Parents have to balance their urge to protect with a willingness to let their child grow by making mistakes. Kids must learn to balance their need for independence with the willingness to take sound advice.

The aim of the examples in this book is to show how to hear what is meant rather than what is being said. The family is the one group we will belong to all our lives. Big or small, it is only as strong as each member, and each must be free to express all their feelings, even ones that aren't nice.

Part One of this book deals with some of the old standby phrases parents often use. It is meant to be read by adolescents. Part Two treats things adolescents would say, and is aimed at parents. But the entire book is really aimed at the whole family. It is to be shared, along with everyone's problems and concerns. There is a very special love between parents and their children. That love is best expressed when there is give and take on both sides. Working as a team makes any task easier. Let's put the time and effort needed into learning how to hear one another. Let's use our hearts as well as our ears.

Part I

When I Was Your Age

When your parents say:
    When I was your age . . .
The hidden meaning is:
    Today's kids have it too easy.

Parents usually use this statement in the wrong spirit. It sounds like the beginning of a lecture and that's a real turn-off.
    "When I was your age . . .
        . . . we walked to school."
        . . . we weren't allowed to date."
        . . . we were never allowed to answer back."
        . . . we had chores to do every day."
    Instead, the phrase could foster understanding, and you can encourage your parents to look at it this way. When a conversation starts with "When I was your age . . . ," figure out if it refers to rules or feelings. The rules you can do without. There are a whole new set of rules today. The feelings you can use:
    "When I was your age . . .
        . . . I worried about how I looked."

. . . I was scared to date."

. . . I needed friends to talk to."

. . . I thought my parents didn't understand."

. . . I wanted to run away sometimes."

Most kids go through these things. It's part of growing up for any generation. Times may have changed, but growing up hasn't. If parents use the benefit of their age in this sense, there is a lot in it for you. Picture your mom worrying about whether or not she's pretty. She did when she was your age. Picture your dad nervous about asking a girl for a date. He was when he was your age. Picture them upset about having pimples. They were! They haven't always been adults. They had to grow up, just like you will, and even if they don't always remember how they did it, they remember how they felt. Ask them.

When your parents say:

I don't know what I'm going to do with you!

The hidden meaning is:

Help!

It's that simple. They need your help. It's easy for family members to become frustrated. Little things that ordinarily wouldn't bother you with friends really get on your nerves when you deal with them every day with family members. There is a saying—"If two rocks sit next to each other long enough, they will get into a fight."

When you were little, your parents could tell you what to do. They had full control over you. As you got older, they lost control but gained cooperation. Your cooperation is needed to keep the family running smoothly.

One reason family life can be difficult is that each member can have slightly different values. Just because your parents raised you doesn't mean you will agree with everything they say. They may want your closet clean. You may think closing the door is enough. They may insist that everyone eat dinner at

6:00. You may be starving at 5:00. They may go to church out of love. You may go because you have to. It is very important that everyone learn to live with each other the way they are.

The day may come when a middle ground has to be reached. Your parents have tried everything they can think of to change your habits and you're still the same. Whatever it is that annoys them won't go away. So what do they do? They throw up their hands and say, "I don't know what I'm going to do with you."

And they don't. They are asking for your help. They feel that they cannot live with a certain habit. Here's your cue to step in. How much are you willing to change? How much time and work will you put into it? How much are your parents willing to accept?

You will all have to decide what you can live with and work toward that goal. It is a goal that must be shared. It isn't just your parents' problem. Anything at home affects the whole family.

When your parents say:
  Just who do you think you are?
The hidden meaning is:
  Don't forget who I am.

Parents have authority over their kids. The older kids get, the less authority parents have. How and when kids begin to acquire increased independence is different in every family. It can be a painful, awkward stage for everyone. Your parents aren't sure how to treat you. Their confusion shows in double messages—they tell you two things at the same time:

- They ask your opinion on some things, but tell you to leave the room during adult conversations.
- They may let you babysit for other kids, but you aren't allowed to stay at home alone.
- They may tell you to use your own judgment, then criticize what you choose.

Some of the roughest areas of miscommunication develop during this time. Parents can't see their kids as anything but their kids. Kids want to be recognized as growing-up people. Tempers flare as everyone fights for position.

How do you learn to be a responsible adult? First you have to handle responsibilities. You have to approach the rest of your life one step at a time. And this particular time is a frightening one for parents.

Your parents have a power over you which they will be afraid to give up. It's the only way they have ever related to you.

When you hear "Just who do you think you are, young lady/man?", you have done something that wasn't expected. Your parents are the ones who aren't sure who you are. You are growing up and demanding new rights. You are challenging their authority over you.

You have to discover what is acceptable behavior now that you are getting older. During a conversation, your parents may expect you to listen without responding. They may consider your answers "talking back." You expect to be able to voice your opinions and feelings.

Look at a situation and figure out what's going on in the family. As family members change, family rules need to change. The whole family is growing up.

When your parents say:
    You're not ready for that yet.
The hidden meaning is:
    We're afraid you'll get hurt.

Your parents' opinion of your abilities will differ from your own at times. Many times that won't matter. Where safety is concerned parents can be very conservative. If they feel you will be in danger, they won't risk letting you try something new.

You may know a family where the kids never seem to have any hassles. They pretty much tell their parents what they will be doing. No arguing, no negotiating, no problems. Why couldn't you have parents like that?

Every family is different, and things are not always as they seem from the outside. What goes on in other families will not often influence your parents' decisions about you. You just have to accept that.

Parents who let their kids do whatever they want are expressing their love in a way you would find hard to live with. You understand your parents' kind of caring best. They care

12

about what you do and who you see. All that caring may seem like interfering, but it's done out of love, not spite.

When your parents say no, it is because, in their judgment, you're not ready to deal with the problems that might arise from something you want to do. They don't want to stop your personal growth, even when it means pain.

Suppose your parents wouldn't let you learn to walk because they knew you'd fall down and get hurt? You'd be a physical cripple today. They guarded you against dangerous falls, but let you stumble a bit and learn on your own. The same is true with your feelings. They don't want you to be an emotional cripple. However, if they see you headed for a dangerous emotional fall, they will step in.

They can't stop your feelings, so they will try to direct you to a solution that is best for you.

When your parents tell you you're not ready, yet, they fully expect you to be ready soon. They know you are growing up.

When your parents say:

I'm older than you and have more experience, so I know what's best for you.

The hidden meaning is:

I've made the same mistakes.

Adults often give the word "experience" a bad name. That's a shame, because it can be so helpful in growing up. People seem to learn best from their own experiences. The lessons are personal, and they stick. But you can't learn everything from experience. You might not survive, and if you did, there is so much to learn that there wouldn't be any time left over to enjoy life.

Older people give advice based on their experiences. You have a choice when it comes to taking advice. You can listen and follow it, listen and not follow it, or not listen at all. Quite often, the way advice is given influences the choice you'll make. That choice could affect the rest of your life.

BORING...

14

When parents see their child headed for trouble, they must step in. To watch and do nothing would be cruel, and they have the power to help avert some pain.

The next time your parents tell you they are older and know better, ask them what they know. This doesn't mean you have to challenge them. Find out what they have seen that makes them think you are making a mistake. This gives you an opportunity to point out differences between that time and now. You could explain how you see the situation. Tell them you have thought about the risks and how you would handle them.

Instead of "I'm older than you . . . " turning into a lecture, it could become a discussion. Once they know you are listening, they will be more likely to talk instead of shout. You'll get a chance to explain your point of view. It works out better for everyone.

When your parents say:
   This is harder on me than it is on you.
The hidden meaning is:
   It hurts me to see you unhappy.

   It doesn't seem to make sense for your parents to punish you and then say the punishment isn't as hard on you as it is on them. That seems like a cheap way to get sympathy.
   It isn't sympathy your parents want, though. It's understanding. They already know that what they are telling you is upsetting. That bothers them. They know how you will react. If there were any way they could get the message across without your anger or pain they would. All their strength to influence you lies in their ability to reason with you. By getting you angry, they lose

that influence. This isn't what they want, but they may be stuck with it.

Parents can't lose sight of who they are. They want and need your friendship, but they are also your guardians. If anything happens to you, it will be their fault, or at least they will blame themselves. If they feel they must do something for your well-being that will anger you, then that's what they must do.

There isn't much time for parents to show their children everything they need to know in order to handle life. Sometimes the lessons are hard. It can be just as hard for the parent to watch as it is for the child to learn. It is hard in different ways, of course, but it still hurts. And your parents love you enough to hurt right along with you.

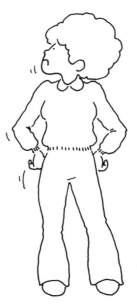

When your parents say:
    Call us tonight so we know where you are.
The hidden meaning is:
    Call us tonight so we know *how* you are.

Sometimes there is nothing so annoying, so inconvenient, so aggravating or embarrassing as stopping whatever you are doing to make a phone call. Looking around for a phone during a party just to "report in" can be a pain. It would be so easy not to bother and just explain when you get home.

Your parents aren't checking up on you. They wouldn't know if you were lying to them over the phone. They aren't trying to ruin your good time. They want to know how you are.

Knowing your whereabouts would be important in case of an accident or emergency. Accidents do happen, not just to other people, but to people you know. You know the whole rap about "What if we need to find you during an emergency?" Well, what if there is one? Could you be found if you were needed?

More important than all of that is how YOU are. A quick call, just a few words, ends all the worry. It also makes it easier for them to trust you if you say you'll call and you do.

The excuse that "I couldn't get to a phone" is only going to work a few times. The way your parents see it, if you don't phone in, you aren't responsible enough to manage yourself.

The usual objection to phoning home is that it will make you look like a little kid to your friends. Think about it. It's little kids who *don't* phone home. Little kids stay out late to play and get in trouble. As a responsible person, you'll let your parents have a general idea of where you expect to be.

Your mom and dad phone each other when their plans change, or just to check in with one another. That's all they want from you. The 60 second phone call tells them you know they worry about you out of love. It shows them you respect that. It tells them how you are.

When your parents say:
    Someday you'll thank me for this:
The hidden meaning is:
    I hope someday you'll understand.

Sounds pretty cruel. How could they ever expect you to thank them when they've hurt you this way?

You can't understand why your parents have told you "no." Seeing an older person's point of view can be impossible at times. It's the age difference. Your parents *were* where you *are*. They see things differently because they have had the time to.

Things have changed in the world, but people haven't changed much. Kids may be a little more sophisticated, but you can only grow up so fast. At times, some things will just go right over your head.

You may know that if you do a certain

thing you'll get in trouble. When you want something so badly that you don't care what happens, you are under the spell of temptation. We've all felt that way. At first your parents may have to resist temptation for you, as they did when you were a baby and your curiosity kept pulling you toward that hot stove or steep stairway. It takes time to be able to say no to your friends when something sounds too good to pass up.

Your parents are telling you that someday you'll realize they were thinking of your future. They were concerned about the long-term effects on you.

It would be much easier for your parents to give in. They love you, and standing up to a loved one is not an easy thing to do. They are willing to do for you what you can't do for yourself yet. They don't expect you to understand now, but maybe someday. . . .

When your parents say:
    You can't have your cake and eat it, too.
The hidden meaning is:
    You can't have everything your own way.

This message isn't really about cake—it's about life. You can't have anything without giving something in exchange. No one can. Sometimes you give, sometimes you take, and there are other people to consider in everything you do. The effect on others is important. This is tough to realize, sometimes. How other people are affected by what you decide is *just as important* as what you want.

    "You can't have your cake and eat it, too" is an overused little phrase. It insults the listener because it sounds so silly. When you hear it, rephrase it in your mind. What your parents are telling you is that you're asking for more than others are willing to give.

    "Hey Mom, could you take me swimming and then pick me up and take me to Carol's house?"

What about Mom? Should she be expected to drive you around all afternoon?

"Hey Dad, could I have the car tonight and tomorrow morning? I need the gas card, too."

Maybe Dad has plans already. Or maybe he'd be willing to loan you the car if you would pay for your own gas.

"Hey Sis, could you loan me $10.00 and take my babysitting job tonight?"

"You can't have your cake and eat it, too" means you'd better go babysit. Make some money and use it to go out another night. What you want now will infringe on others. You can have what you want, but on different terms.

It takes a mature person to look at the benefits and drawbacks of a situation, before deciding the best thing to do. It takes a mature person to look at a piece of cake and then wait until it's time to eat.

When your parents say:
   Stay away from those kids. They are trouble.
The hidden meaning is:
   We don't want you getting into trouble.

   Parents have a way of saying things that get you so angry you refuse to listen to them. They lose the one thing they want— your attention. The problem isn't what they are saying. It's the way they say it. Don't hold that against them. They are probably too worried to think straight.
   Your parents don't always tell you who to see or not see. Why now? What have they heard? Do they have a valid reason to be concerned?
   Look at your friends the way they are most of the time, not just when they are on good behavior to impress someone. Most of your friends are just fine. But there are the sly ones.
   Certain kids are "headed for trouble." You need to look at that, especially if you like them. The chronic school skipper, the liar, the kid who thinks all that matters is a Good Time—they have some value problems. No reason not to like them; every reason not to

trust them. To be a friend and have a friend there must be trust. Don't be foolish enough to put your trust into a people-user.

Your parents don't want you getting into trouble. The chances of that happening if you associate with troublemakers are pretty good. As you get older there are higher consequences for mistakes. Legally and morally a lot more is expected of you. The rest of your life could change because of a mistake in your teens. A criminal record, a pregnancy, a drug habit; these problems will follow you through life. Your parents know that. They are scared for you.

Out of their fear comes the need to protect you. When they see you headed for trouble don't expect them to sit by. They will pry, interfere, nag—whatever they think it takes. Expect it, don't resent it.

If your parents are misinformed, it's your responsibility to straighten this out. If the friendship is important, you'll have to find a way to save it. It will take work and cooperation with your parents.

If your parents were wrong in their judgment they will admit it.

Will you?

Part II
I'm Not A Baby Any More

When your child says:
 I hate you!
The hidden meaning is:
 You hurt me.

There is a fine line between feeling emotional hurt and feeling hate. It takes a mature person to accept a personal blow gracefully. Kids don't have that maturity. They haven't had time to develop it. Hurt their feelings deeply enough and with red face and teary eyes they will lash out "I hate you!"

It's a defense, a reflex action to protect them from more hurt. They feel cornered and they strike out.

It doesn't end there. Soon after this outburst, as anger ebbs, guilt flows in. Your child cringes over having said taboo words to a parent. It is the closest thing to a curse there is. You *never* tell your parents you hate them. (What if they die?!)

You are the adult. It is up to you to settle this fight. Keep the argument personal. So often one parent runs to the aid of the other. Three people end up battling instead of two. This is no time to gang up. There is nothing earth-shattering about a healthy fight between a parent and child. Don't take it too seriously.

A first step in settling the fight could be to counter the anger with love. When you hear

28

the shout "I hate you!" calmly answer "I'm sorry you're hurting right now. I love you." To stop a war, all you have to do is not supply ammunition.

If the situation is too volatile, just sit and let some time pass so your child won't feel cornered. Don't forget—after yelling at you, your child figures he or she is in big trouble now. Let the comment fade away. It wasn't meant, anyway.

Always remember what the argument is about. Stick to the issue. Countering with "How dare you talk back to me!" doesn't solve the original problem. What upset the child? As more issues arise during your talk, always return to the starting point. Solve one problem at a time.

Your child has always loved you. That love can't be wiped out in one heated argument, or even a dozen. However, with each hurt, communication and closeness can break down a little. Help your child work past the pain and guilt. It is more important to communicate when angry than at any other time. Don't let your child withdraw in guilt and shame. You may not like what he or she feels, but that doesn't mean it isn't important. For a family to survive, *all* feelings have to be expressed, even the ones that aren't nice.

When your child says:
    You don't like any of my friends.
The hidden meaning is:
    All you do is criticize.

Friendships are very important to adolescents. Outside of the immediate family, friends are the strongest support group your child will have. They share and swap and tell secrets. They spend more time together than they do with their families.

Friends choose each other. This commitment is special because it is voluntary. Friends extend and expand your child's own personality. They copy what they admire about each other.

Your objection to a friendship is taken personally. In effect, you belittle your child's judgment. Your child may be trying to be like the very person you object to and may naturally be protective of that friend.

You may have valid insights into the

HSSSST!

friendships your child has. To be accepted, that information must be presented in a non-threatening way. Be constructive, not critical, and you will have an interested audience.

Balance the good with the bad. Most adults say nothing if they have no complaints, but your child needs to know when things are good as well as bad. When he or she doesn't hear anything from you, it indicates you don't care or don't listen.

Most kids disappear from the friendship list as fast as they appear. Save your energy by ignoring fleeting friendships. You may get the chance to have your *informed* opinion heard once. Save your breath until then and make it count.

Your thoughts are important. Your child will be looking for your approval in almost anything he or she does. Remember how important your *good* opinion is. Don't use that power sparingly. Heap it on.

31

When your child says:

Why can't I smoke? You do.

The hidden meaning is:

Why are there two sets of rules?

Do as I say, not as I do. That is a well-intentioned but futile expression. People follow example. Demonstration is the quickest way to teach a lesson. By the time your child reaches adolescence, he or she knows how to behave. Your child has watched you through the most impressionable years.

Do you smoke? Do you drink? Your child has reached an age where he or she feels qualified for some adult privileges, too.

If you or your mate smokes there is a strong chance your child will follow your example. Lectures to the contrary won't help much. You can't puff on a cigarette and talk about lung cancer. Your child won't listen

because if cancer were really a risk you would stop smoking, right?

The same goes for other behaviors as well. If you don't want your children to drink or use other drugs, if you don't want them to be disrespectful of property or to drive recklessly or to mistreat others, you must set the example by your actions.

If your child is looking for ways to show maturity, offer some. Later curfews, larger allowances; any privileges which show that you see your child is growing up will fill this need.

We don't have much time to prepare our children for the adult world. We jeopardize the quality of that time by sending conflicting messages. For a message to have meaning and power, the words must be backed by action. If you say it, mean it. If you mean it, do it.

When your child says:
    Get off my back!
The hidden meaning is:
    Stop pressuring me. I need room to deal with this.

Whenever you hear "Get off my back," picture this: See a young kid being relentlessly ridden until he or she says what a parent wants to hear.

Think about it. Stop riding the child. Your child has a problem that bothers *you*. You want to know what it is so you can solve it and everything can be nice again.

In a battle of wills there is no winner. You may get the information or behavior you're after, but not a resolution. Your goal—the healthy growth of your child—is much broader. In the heat of an argument it is easy to lose sight of that. Whatever your child is withholding isn't what is ultimately important.

As a parent, you will not be first choice in many confidences your child shares. That's what friends are for. It's an important step in growing up. It's not that you are being *excluded*. Your child is *including* others.

At times you will sense your child is holding back. You know something is bothering him or her. You imagine the worst and you worry.

Let your child know that you sense trouble. Let him or her know you are always available to talk. Then wait. Timing is important. There is a fine line between being a nag and being concerned.

If you believe your child is headed toward physical harm, intervene. If it is a matter of emotional confusion, let it work itself out. You're probably more uncomfortable than the child is. But the problem can't be solved for your comfort. It must be resolved for his or her well-being.

No one likes to see someone they love suffer. At times it may be unavoidable. Pain moves people to action. Your child won't suffer forever. He or she will do whatever they can to work through this. Give your child room to work things out. While you may not get to share the problem, you will share the answer. And the child will grow.

When your child says:
    Forget it. It's not important.
The hidden meaning is:
    You don't want to hear this.

Parents look for ways to establish open, honest communication with their children.

You ask your child to trust you. You tell him or her to come to you with problems. You even yell when he or she doesn't. But first you let your child know what you don't want to hear:

— Don't ever let me find out . . . .
— Don't ever let me hear . . . .
— I'd better not ever catch you . . . .
— My child would never . . . .

Guess what your child hears? You don't want to know about certain problems. You've threatened your child. The unspoken punishment hangs in the air. A child would rather suffer silently than surrender to the threat.

One way to turn your child off is to say "Didn't I tell you . . . ?" Children know

FORGET IT!

when they are going to get yelled at and they tune parents right out. What they need is someone to listen.

Your child needs to learn ways out of situations. There is no doubt he or she will get into a fair share of trouble. Prepare your child, don't threaten.

Discuss subjects BEFORE your child becomes self-conscious about them. For example, talking to a fifteen-year-old about the facts of life will be awkward and probably too late.

Establish high values for your child by your own example. Be careful not to establish high expectations. Your child will do some very foolish things due to inexperience. Go through the situation and find out where his or her judgment was off. Allow your child time to rethink failures.

If listening is done with humility and not humiliation your family will become stronger, healthier, and closer.

When your child says:
  I've tried smoking pot.
The hidden meaning is:
  What do I do now?

Smoking pot is not something kids first try alone. There are influences they must face everyday. Friends, parties, and even relatives may praise pot as some kind of wonder drug. Add this to peer pressure to conform and your child is a sitting duck when a group gathers.

Being well-informed as to the latest research on marijuana will help your child resist pressures to smoke with their friends. But children need more than that. They must value their bodies and minds more than the opinion of a few friends. That's not easy for a teenager.

Developing a healthy attitude towards life begins at home. Having the strength to stand by convictions and believe in your values must be taught through example. Parents must help their children not be vulnerable to their friends to the point of being victims.

When all is said and done, your child makes the final decisions on friends and

smoking pot. All you can do is guide, but one thing is basic. Parents can either deny or confront this situation. Denial pushes it under the surface. It's a boil that will someday erupt. Confrontation is painful, but that boil can drain and heal. Your family will change. It will never be the same again. It can be better. You will have to be daring enough to question and search, and to do so with love and understanding.

Check your older children. Many times youngsters get "turned on" to smoking by older siblings. Question *every* family member.

Every family is unique. There is no single answer. To arrive at the answer for your particular family:

1. Get all the information you can.
2. Face the facts. Don't rationalize them away.
3. If the child is doing more than just experimenting and refuses to stop, get professional help *for the family*.

It may take a couple of visits. It may take a year. But being a family is a lifetime proposition.

When your child says:
    Don't you trust me?
The hidden meaning is:
    Give me a chance.

This question demands a straight yes or no answer. You have been asked directly, "Don't you trust me?" Answer directly.

It's okay to say "No, you lied to me recently and I'm not sure if you're lying now." Let your child defend and explain. There is no reason for you to be defensive. The responsibility rests with your child.

If there is a reason for you to doubt your child, say so. Get it out in the open. Maybe all you have are vague fears. Giving your child a chance at new situations will either confirm or dismiss these fears.

It may not be a matter of trust. A fifteen-year-old, wanting to go to an unchaperoned party for 15- to 18-year-olds, may say, "Don't you trust me?" It is a dangerous situation. There will be little, if any, control over

the party. Your child can't be trusted to make it a safe party. It already isn't.

This is a matter of protecting, not trusting. Parents naturally want to protect their children from harm. Your child sees your actions as stifling. Explain the difference. You have confidence in him or her but you have some real concerns about this particular situation.

Through the adolescent years your child needs opportunities to show you his or her ability to deal with the adult world. More than that, an adolescent needs to prove growth to him- or herself. Provide opportunities for that. Start small and work up. Ease into adulthood.

At some point you will have to take your hands off, voluntarily or otherwise. You can't trust someone you never give freedom to.

Watching your child take risks and get hurt is painful. The reward is in growing up.

When your child says:
    I'm not a baby anymore.
The hidden meaning is:
    Let me grow up.

Welcome to the post-child, pre-adult world. Nothing typifies that stage more than the need to be independent.

How you handle this need makes the difference between conflict and cooperation. Conflict develops if your child feels trapped in the stale role of "my baby." Cooperation develops when your child feels recognized as a potential adult.

There will be many opportunities for your teenager to grow. Kids don't live in a vacuum. They've picked up information that would amaze you. They just need a chance to use it responsibly.

How much growing has your child done? Provide opportunities at home for him or her to show you. Let your child plan a party. He or she must organize the affair—invitations, refreshments, entertainment, clean-up. All you do is chaperone. Keep your hands off

42

the project. Sure, you could do better, but that's not the point. Your adolescent must learn to begin *and* finish projects. You won't always be there to clean up afterwards.

There is a tug of war going on within your teenager: the need for security vs. the need for independence. Teenagers are intellectually ready to cope with growing up before they are ready emotionally. Your guidance can balance the intellect with the emotions. They must learn that needing help doesn't have to threaten independence.

Demanding or expecting results brings on rebellion. No one likes to be ordered around. If children feel nothing short of perfection will do, their world will shrink. They will attempt only sure endeavors. That way there is no failure, no criticism, no growth.

Recognize your teenager as a growing-up person. Treat him or her the way you would want to be treated. Show your love for who your child is *now*, not for who he or she will become.

When your child says:
  I wish I were dead.
The hidden meaning is:
  I'm depressed.

No matter what the circumstances are surrounding this comment, DO NOT ignore it.
Many myths surround suicide:
- People who talk about suicide don't do it.
- Suicide "attempts" are not meant to succeed.
- You'd know if someone close to you were contemplating suicide.

All of those statements are false.

People, even teenagers, talk about suicide because they are thinking about it. It is a possible alternative for them. While it isn't a definite decision, the idea is there.

Suicide attempts are not the ploy of spoiled attention-getters. They have reached the end of their endurance. A successful suicide means the end of it all. Failure gives others a chance to intervene and help.

People we love do kill themselves, many times without warning. If any signals were sent, only hindsight reveals them. Many people hide their inner turmoil behind a facade of normalcy. They explain away signs of depression as fatigue, hunger, or a need to get away for a while. We've all felt that way, so we accept it.

Depression, left untreated, is as serious for children as it is for adults. Many times children are left to handle all this alone. No one takes their problems seriously because of their age.

Family troubles are taken extremely hard by teenagers and pre-teens. Low self-esteem, insecurity, fear of failure—these all contribute to a child's feelings of worthlessness.

Be alert to any changes in your child's normal patterns. Withdrawal from friends, neglect of favorite hobbies, a drop in grades, and loss of appetite or energy are some signs.

As the parent, you will not be able to help when objectivity is needed. You are too close to the situation. You may unknowingly be part of the problem. Try to talk to your child, then let others who are not emotionally involved take over.

However powerless you may feel, the one thing you *can* do is seek professional guidance. And it must be immediate, even if you find it difficult to go outside the family for help. After all, the stakes are life and death.

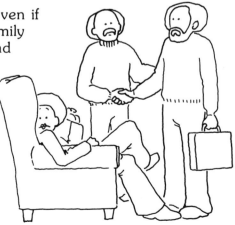

Conclusion

The child we all once were is still alive within us. We need to remember that. As parents, we should remember how powerful the emotions of the child can be, and how natural is the drive for independence. As children, we should remind ourselves that our parents still see that child in us, no matter how our bodies change and grow.

Let's accept the challenge to know one another as a family. The opportunity is there. All we have to do, each of us, is listen. It takes a little effort and a lot of practice, but so do all worthwhile skills. When emotions are running high, the challenge is greater, but so are the rewards. And the rewards are serenity, self-esteem, and a lifetime of love, understanding, and support from those who know us best.